수줍은 댕댕이 눈빛

Shy Glance of My Lovely Puppy

수줍은 댕댕이 눈빛
(Shy Glance of My Lovely Puppy)
심재황 제6시집 (한영시집)

2023년 5월 30일 제 1판 인쇄 발행

지 은 이 ｜ 심재황
펴 낸 이 ｜ 심재황
펴 낸 곳 ｜ 도서출판 나리북스

등록번호 ｜ 2023-000001 (2022년 02월 08일)
주 소 ｜ 15802 경기도 군포시 고산로 677번길 34, 1324-1303
대표전화 ｜ 031) 398-5610
팩 스 ｜ 031) 398-5610
이 메 일 ｜ julyshim@hanmail.net
ISBN 979-11-979286-2-8 (03800)
가격 11,000원

※ 잘못 만들어진 책은 바꿔드립니다.
이 책 내용의 일부 또는 전부를 재사용하려면
반드시 저작권자의 동의를 받아야 합니다.

수줍은 댕댕이 눈빛
Shy Glance of My Lovely Puppy

심재황 제6시집 (한영시집)
Jaehwang Shim

도서출판 나리북스

시인의 말

강아지를 데리고 왔어요. 그 전에 몇 번 보았던 강아지입니다. 꼬마 시절에 발발거리고 뒹굴던 모습이 조금 무디고, 표정도 변한 것 같았어요.

집으로 데리고 들어오자마자 여기저기 돌아다니며 무척이나 즐거워했어요. 한 구석으로 가보고 나를 쳐다보고, 저쪽에서 냄새 맡아보고 나를 쳐다보고, 소파에 뛰어오르고 나를 쳐다보고. 우리 함께 잘 지내보자고 합니다.

이제 이곳이 자기 자리이니 남들은 얼씬거리지 말라고 합니다. 아파트 문밖에 누구라도 지나가면 바로 경계하고, 조금 떨어진 엘리베이터 오르내리는 소리에도 경계합니다.

한동안 얼굴을 마주치지 않으면, 앞발로 내 옆구리를 건드립니다. 자기를 보아주던지, 아니면 안아달라고 하면서.

주로 봄과 여름에 강아지를 데리고 다니며 느낀 글입니다. 여기에서 강아지, 강쥐, 댕댕이, 꼬물이, 애리 … 모두 한 마리 "애리"입니다. 하얀 바탕에 귀와 등에 연한 크림색이 드리운 포메라이언(Pomeranian) 강아지입니다.

성별도 내용에 따라서 바꾸어 보았지만(She, He, It), "애리" 한 마리입니다. 사랑하는 애리의 수줍은 눈빛을 보면서 이야기를 꾸며 보았습니다.

2023년 5월

A Poet's Foreword

I brought my dog I had seen a few times before. The way he used to roar and roll around, when he was a kid, has become a bit dull.

As soon as he came home, he was very happy to walk around here and there looking at me: going to a corner, sniffing from the other side, jumping on the couch, and wishing to get along well with me.

Now that this is his place, he tells others not to wander around. If anyone passes outside the door, he is immediately alert.

If I don't see his face for a while, his front paw touches my side: hoping to look at himself or asking for a hug.

Here, Puppy, Gang-gee, Daengdaengi, Kkomulee, and Aery are all one. It's a Pomeranian puppy with a light cream color on a white background.

I changed the gender depending on the content (She, He, It), but it is only one "Aery". I made up stories feeling the black eyes of my beloved Aery.

May, 2023

차례

1부 벚꽃 댕댕이

A Cherry Puppy

12 댕댕이 벚꽃 Cherry Blossoms
14 조용한 밤비 Quiet Rain at Night
16 저녁 조팝꽃 Bridal Wreath at Sunset
18 자기 자리 A Puppy's Place
22 초여름 들어서 Early Summer
24 민들레와 송이 얼굴 The Dandelion Face
26 샘가 새끼 고라니 A Baby Roe Deer
28 우울한 저녁 비 Gloomy Evening Rain
30 무당벌레 청소기 A Ladybug Cleaner
32 한밤에 자라고 Growing Up at Night
34 부러운 강아지 A Happy Puppy
36 민들레 솜털 Dandelion Fluff
38 건물 사이 자리 A Space in Buildings

차례

40 한낮 습기 The Midday Humidity
42 겁먹은 고라니 A Scared Roe Deer
44 홀로 앉은 분 Sitting Alone in the Yard

2부 피곤한 댕댕이

A Tired Puppy

48 꼬물이 다듬기 Trimming Puppy's Hair
50 꼬물이 목욕 Bathing a Puppy
52 넓적다리 베개 A Thigh Pillow
54 비빔밥 세 그릇 Three Bowls of Bibimbap
56 강아지 음식 The Puppy's Foods
58 늦은 간식 Late Snack
60 강아지 바나나 Puppy's Banana
62 그리운 송이 언니 Missing My Sister

차례

66 강아지 비 Puppy Rain
68 젖은 손수레 A Wet Cart
70 한밤중 빗소리 Raining at Midnight
72 갑자기 더위 A Sudden Heat
74 복숭아 색깔 The Peach Color
76 무더위 소리 The Sound of Heat
78 지친 강아지 A Tired Puppy
82 가을바람 강아지 A Puppy in Fall

3부 우울한 댕댕이

A Blue Puppy

86 우울한 눈빛 The Blue Glance
90 댕댕이 걍걍걍 The Puppy Noises
92 장대비 근심 An Anxious Rain
94 늦은 밤 언니 방 A Room at Midnight

차례

96 기다란 목과 다리 Long Neck and Legs
98 꼬물이 찔끔 Making a Little Pee
100 다시 집으로 Back Home
102 크림색 별 A Cream Colored Star
104 불안한 아기 An Anxious Baby
106 거실을 나가며 Leaving the Living Room
108 빗방울 소리 The Raindrops
110 짙어지는 계절 The Thick Color
112 아름다운 모습 A Beautiful Look
114 우울한 과거 Gloomy Past Memories
116 기다림 Waiting for Someone
118 장마 코스모스 A Cosmos in Rain
120 가을 풀벌레 Autumn Bugs
122 함께 가기로 Going Together
124 댕댕이 이발기 A Hair Clipper
126 댕댕이 미용 The Puppy Grooming
128 외로운 댕댕이 A Lonely Puppy

수줍은 댕댕이 눈빛

Shy Glance of My Lovely Puppy

1부

벚꽃 댕댕이

댕댕이 벚꽃

봄바람이 불어오면
하얀 벚꽃이 날려서
댕댕이 머리에 떨어져요.

날리는 벚꽃 송이를
우두커니 바라보다가

화려한 벚꽃 속으로
댕댕이는 들어가요

하얀 벚꽃에 둘러싸여
까만 눈과 까만 코만
조그맣게 반짝여요.

Cherry Blossoms

As the spring wind blows,
Flying cherry blossoms
Falls on the puppy's head.

A puppy is staring at
The flying cherry blossoms.

He is slowing going
Into the colorful blossoms.

Surrounded by white blossoms
Black eyes and a black nose
Are only glittering.

조용한 밤비

한밤중이 너무 조용하여
창밖을 살펴보니

이미 한참 동안이나
비가 내리고 있는데

새벽이 되어서
누가 알아차릴까봐.

한밤중에 소리도 없이
서둘러서 내리고 있는데

강아지가 창가에서
가만히 듣고 있어요.

Quiet Rain at Night

Midnight is so quiet,
Near the window side

Already for a long while
It's been raining.

When it gets dawn,
Avoiding someone's noticing,

It hurries down silently
In the middle of the night.

A puppy at the window
Is listening to the raindrops.

저녁 조팝꽃

어디에 가다 보면
하얀색 있다고 하는데

소나무 사이에 떨어지는
함박눈이 있는데

해질 무렵에 흔들리는
조팝꽃 무리를 보면서

새하얀 색 이라고 하는지
새하얀 빛 이라고 하는지

Bridal Wreath

Wherever you go,
They say it's white

Between the pines
Falling big snowballs.

Looking at the bunches of
White bridal wreath
Waving at sunset,

Are they pure white color?
Are they pure white light?

자기 자리

이제 미루지 말아야 하기에
오늘 강아지를 데리고 왔어요.

이전에 몇 번 본적이 있기에
강아지는 나를 보자마자
한 번에 달려들어서 안겨요.

집 안으로 들이오자마자
문 안에 내려놓자마자
여기저기 화다닥 뛰어다니고

강아지 물건을 배치해 두고
자리를 정해 주려고 하는데

강아지는 이미 집안 구석구석
자기 영역으로 지정해 놓아요.

큰방과 작은방을 들락거리며
현관에서 거실을 지나서

베란다까지 바람처럼 달리며
자기 운동장으로 만들어요.

소파에 껑충 뛰어 올라가서
한바탕 뒹굴고 뒹굴어요.

A Puppy's Place

Because I can't delay it anymore
I brought the puppy today.

'Cause I've seen it a few times before
As soon as the pomeranian sees me,
Runs at once and hugs in my arms.

As soon as it enters my place,
And I put it down in the floor,
It's running all over the place.

I try to prepare for something basic
Trying to arrange a seat,

The puppy already designates its area
Everywhere in the house.

Going in and out of the rooms,
From the entrance to the sitting room,

Running like the wind to the veranda,
It makes all house its own playground.

Jumping up on the sofa
Rolling around and rolling around.

초여름 들어서

한 달 동안이나
기다리고 기다려서
봄을 맞이하였더니

사흘 동안 봄꽃은
여기저기 만발하더니

오늘 하루 만에
봄꽃은 떨어지고

오늘이 가기 전에
초여름이 찾아오고

오늘 반나절 안에
초여름 길로 들어가고

Early Summer

For a month or so
Having been waiting and
Waiting for spring,

For three days in a row,
Flowers bloom everywhere

Today, however, in one day
Spring flowers fall down.

Before the end of today,
Early summer is coming

Within half a day today
Entering the path of summer.

민들레와 송이 얼굴

민들레 피어날 때가 되면
햇살이 따갑고

햇살 받은
민들레 얼굴은 샛노랗고

햇살 받은
송이 얼굴은 까무잡잡하고

민들레는 봄볕에 그을려도
그대로 노란색인데

송이는 봄볕에 살짝 닿아도
얼굴색이 검게 변해지고

민들레는 송이를 바라보고
송이는 민들레를 바라보고

The Dandelion Face

When the dandelion blooms,
The sun is hot.

The face of a dandelion sunlit
Is bright yellow,

Songhee's face, a little girl, sunlit
Is getting dark.

The dandelion scorched
By the spring sun is still yellow.

A little girl's face lightly touched
By the spring sun turns dark.

The dandelion looks at the girl;
She looks at the dandelion.

샘가 새끼 고라니

무성한 샛길에 들어가서
하늘이 보이지 않아요.

수풀에서 새끼 고라니가
저쪽 비탈로 뛰어가요.

오리나무 아래 샘가를
힌걸음에 뛰어넘어서

저쪽 비탈로 뛰어서
덤불 속으로 들어가요.

저기 흔들리는 억새 속에서
가만히 엎드려 있나 본데

어미 고라니를 기다리는지
이 근처에 있기로 했는지

A Baby Roe Deer

Enter the lush byway
I can't see the sky.

A baby roe deer in the bush
Runs to that slope.

By the spring under the alder
Jumping over one step,
Jumping down that slope,
It runs into the bush.

In the swaying silver grass,
It may still lie down,

Waiting for a mother deer,
Promising to wait near here.

우울한 저녁 비

저녁에 비 내리고
어두움이 드리워지면
서글픔 일어나기도 하지요.

나 보다 그가 우선 이었고
그의 기쁨을 나는 바랬는데
이제는 나의 슬픔이 남았어요.

비 내리는 저녁이면
나에게 슬픔이 내려와요.

어두움 속에서 비 내리고
나에게 외로움이 남아요.

Gloomy Evening Rain

On a rainy evening,
As darkness falls,
Sadness will happen.

He was more important than me,
His joy was my wish,
Now my sadness remains.

On a rainy evening,
Sadness descends on me.

It's raining in the dark,
Loneliness remains in me.

무당벌레 청소기

빨간 머리 진공청소기는
윙윙 윙윙 소리 내면서

두 눈을 번쩍번쩍 거리며
먼지를 말끔히 빨아들여요.

강아지는 어리벙벙하여
놀라서 슬슬 피해 다녀요.

무당벌레 진공청소기는
이 방 저 방을 돌아다니며
먼지를 먹는 소리를 내고

강아지는 앙큼앙큼 다가와서
앞발로 톡톡 치기도 하면서
양양 짖으며 쫓아다녀요.

A Ladybug Cleaner

Redhead vacuum cleaner
Is buzzing and buzzing.

With both eyes twinkling
It is sucking up the dust.

A puzzled puppy is surprised
And slowly avoiding it.

The ladybug vacuum cleaner
Is moving from room to room
Makes dust eating noises.

The puppy slowly comes closer,
Tapping it with a front foot,
Barking and chasing after it.

한밤에 자라고

사방이 고요하고
밤안개 드리우고
달빛을 받게 되면

심어놓은 작물은
살며시 자라나요.

새벽에 이슬 맞고
살며시 자라나요.

한낮에 가만히 쉬다가도
한밤중에 가만히 자라요.

Growing Up at Night

Everywhere is quiet,
Casting night fog
With the moonlight.

Crops planted
Are growing up softly.

In the morning dew,
The crops grow softly

Resting quietly in the day,
Growing up quietly at night.

부러운 강아지

코로나 때문에 마스크를 쓰는데
외출에서 먼저 챙기는 물건인데

어디에 들어가든지
어디에 앉아있던지
그 누구를 만나던지
꼭 착용해야 하는 물건이 되었어요.

여름에도 답답하지만
산책길에서도 마스크 쓰는데

강아지는 입을 헐떡거리면서
마스크를 쓰지 않아요

산책길에서 강아지가 쳐다봐요.
사람들은 얼마나 답답할까.

A Happy Puppy

Because of Corona virus season,
Wearing a face mask is essential
Whenever you go out.

Wherever you go,
Where you are sitting,
Whoever you meet,
It has become a must-have.

It's stuffy even in summer;
You wear a mask even on a walk.

However, a puppy is panting,
But it doesn't wear a mask.

Staring at you on a walkway,
A puppy says you are really stuffy
Wearing a face mask on.

민들레 솜털

하얀 민들레 솜털은
어디로 날아갔는지
꽃술대 하나만 남아있어요.

솜털이 멀리 날아가면
더 많은 민들레 꽃들이
멀리서 피어난다고 해요.

송이는 민들레 솜털을 들고서
흔들어서 날려 보내요.

입으로 불어서 날려 보내고
손으로 흔들어 날려 보내고
솜털이 보이지 않을 때까지

Dandelion Fluff

White dandelion fluff;
Where it flew away to
There's one flower stalk left.

When the fluff flies away
More dandelion flowers
May bloom from far away.

A little girl holds a fluff,
Shakes, and blows it away.

Blowing it with her mouth,
Shaking it with her hand,
Until she can't see the fluff.

건물 사이 자리

건물 사이로 불어오는 바람은
방향을 구별하지 않아요.

점심시간 이맘때쯤에
어디에서 불어와도 선선해요.

건물과 건물 사이 그늘에
앉을 만힌 자리민 있으면
쉽게 일어나지 못하지요.

커피 들고 지나는 사람들도
앉을 만한 자리를 찾아요.

이리저리 서성이면서
앉을 만한 자리를 찾아요.

A Space in Buildings

The wind through the buildings
Doesn't tell the direction.

Lunchtime around this time,
No matter where it blows,
The wind is usually cool.

In the shade between buildings,
If there's a place to sit on
I can't get up to leave easily.

People passing by bring coffee
Are finding a place to sit on.

While wandering around,
They're fining a place to sit on.

한낮 습기

낮에는 어디에도 습기 덮여서
건물 모퉁이까지 무덥고
나무 그늘도 서늘하지 않아요.

이번 주 매일 매일 흐리겠고
비 내린다는 소식은 없었지만
그게 아니기를 바라기만 해요.

이런 무더위가 얼마나 가는지
바로 맑아지지는 않을 거예요.

거리에도 밭에도 어디에도
한바탕 비 쏟아지기만 바라죠.

The Midday Humidity

During the day, everywhere
Is covered with moisture.

Heating of the corner of the building,
Even the shade of a tree is not cool.

It'll be cloudy every day this week,
There's no news of rain
Though I hope it won't be.

How long does this heat last?
It won't be clear right away.
On the streets, in the fields,
Everywhere should be shed in rain.

겁먹은 고라니

긴 발 가진 고라니는
늘 긴장하여 주위를 살펴요.

들개 승냥이 오소리 담비 멧돼지
언제 들이닥칠지 모르죠.

밤새도록 덤불 더미 속에서
웅그리며 벌벌 떨며 지내기에
한숨조차 나오지 않아요.

들개에게 모가지 물리고
승냥이 발톱에 할퀴고
오소리 머리에 받치고
담비에게 콧등 깨물리고
멧돼지에게 어깨 찔려서

간신히 살아남기도 했어요.

A Scared Roe Deer

A roe deer with long legs
Always looks around nervously.

She doesn't know to face
A wild dog, a hound badger,
A marten, and a wild boar.

All night in a pile of bush,
Crouching and Shivering herself,
It's hard to breathe, even a sigh.

Bitten on the neck by a wild dog,
Clawed by a wolf's claws,
Hit on the side by a badger's head,
Bitten on nose by a sable's teeth,
Stabbed in the shoulder by a wild boar,
She barely saves her life many times.

홀로 앉은 분

사람들이 거닐기에
그 길로 따라갔어요.

사람들이 점점 늘어나서
샛길로 들어갔어요.

하얀 집 마당에 어르신이
하얀 모자를 쓰고서
가만히 앉아 있어요.

한참 샛길을 가다가
너무 한적하여 다시 돌아와요.

아까 그 집이 보이고
그 어르신은 여전히 앉아서
여기 샛길을 내려다보는데
지팡이를 두 손으로 잡고서

Sitting Alone in the Yard

For people to walk through,
I followed the path.

Following more and more people
I went down the path.

An old man wearing a white hat
In the yard of a white house
Is still sitting there.

After going down the other path,
I'm back to the previous path.

In the house I have seen
The old man is still sitting
Looking down the path
Holding his staff with both hands.

2부

피곤한 댕댕이
A Tired Puppy

꼬물이 다듬기

꼬물이 긴 털을 잘라야 하는데
겨울 동안 자라난 털을 자르는데

미용 작업대 위에 엉거주춤 서서
앉지 못하고 불안해 합니다.

먼저 등 위를 한번 쭉 밀어내고
양쪽 뒷다리와 앞다리를 다듬고
무성한 목 아래를 쓸어내려요.

그다음 뒷다리를 멀쭉 세우고서
가슴과 배를 살살 다듬어 주고서
머리와 귀에 난 잔털을 손질해요.

Trimming Puppy's Hair

The puppy, Kkomul, needs to trim
His long hair growing in winter.

Standing on the workbench
He can't sit down, feel uneasy.

First, cut the upper back once,
Trim both hind and forelimbs,
Sweep down the lush neck.

Then, straightening his hind legs
Gently trimming the chest and belly,
And fine hair on the head and ears.

꼬물이 목욕

욕조에 세워두고 미지근한 물에
세제 거품 버무려서 목욕해요.

건조기 통 안에서 털을 말리는데
어서 꺼내 달라며 낑낑거립니다.

빗질하며 삐져나온 털을 다듬으니
완전히 외계인 강아지로 되었어요.

작고 동그란 밤톨 머리에다가
다리가 반 뼘이나 길어 보여요.

어기적 어기적 펄쩍 뛰어다니며
긴 다리 뻗으며 기지개 피네요.

Bathing a Puppy

Placing in a bathtub of warm water,
Taking a bath with detergent foam.

Drying hair in a dryer box,
The puppy whines asking me
To take him out quickly.

Combing, trimming the protruding hair,
The puppy becomes an alien one.

With a small, round chestnut head,
The legs look half a span long.

Jumping around, jumping around
He stretches out his long legs.

넓적다리 베개

소파 한쪽에 기대어서
한 발은 소파 등에 붙이고
한 발을 길게 뻗으면

강아지는 훌쩍 뛰어올라서
두 다리 사이에 자리 잡아요.

길게 뻗은 나의 넓적다리에
자기의 앞발을 얹어두어요.

잠시 후에 넓적다리 위에
자기의 머리를 베고 누워요.

넓적다리는 점점 따스해지고
강아지는 살며시 잠들어가요.

A Thigh Pillow

Leaning on one side of the sofa,
Putting one foot on the sofa,
I extend one leg on the bottom.

The puppy immediately jumps up
And sits between my legs.

On my outstretched thigh,
He puts his front paws.

On the thigh, after a while,
He lies down with his head down.

The thigh is getting warmer
As the puppy is softly asleep.

비빔밥 세 그릇

그런대로 바람은 불지만
무더위를 날리지 못해요

카페 앞 탁자에서
세 분이 앉아서 비빔밥을 드시는데

바로 옆집 식당에서
얼마 전에 새로 마련한 메뉴입니다.

무더위를 잊을 수 있는
시원한 점심을 드시면서
무슨 대화를 나누시는데

정겨운 웃음이 멀리서도 보여요.

Three Bowls of Bibimbap

Even the wind blowing gently
It can't beat the heat.

At the table in front of the cafe
The three gentlemen are sitting
Eating bibimbap, the mixed rice.

This is a new recent dish
At the restaurant next dor.

Forgetting the summer heat
Having a cool lunch of dish
They're talking about themselves.

The friendly smiles can be seen.

강아지 음식

옛날에 강아지와 우리는
먹는 음식이 서로 같아서
성격도 서로 비슷하다고 했어요.

이제는 음식이 서로 다르기에
강아지는 다른 음식을 먹어요.

강아지는 우리와 다르게 먹는데
성격이 다르면 어쩌나 걱정되요.

그런데 강아지에게 간식을 주는데
강아지는 나도 조금 먹어보라고

내 손에 슬쩍 떨어뜨려 주면서
우리끼리 다르지 않다고 하네요.

The Puppy's Foods

Once upon a time, dogs and men
Almost ate the same foods,
We almost had similar personalities.

As time passes, foods are different,
Puppies eat different foods.

Because of difference of foods,
I would be seriously worried
If our personalities may differ.

Then when I give the dog **treats**.
The puppy gives some back to me.

He gently drops it into my hand
Saying we're not different.

늦은 간식

늦은 귀가 길에 애리를 생각해요.

애리는 거실 소파에서 기다리는데
그나마 거실 커튼을 열어 두어서
큰 창문에서 불빛이 들어오기에

거실은 아주 캄캄하지는 않겠으나
검은 눈에 걱정과 두려움이 있어요.

반가워하는 애리에게 주려고
간식을 봉지에 두 겹으로 싸매어
주머니에 넣어두고 있어요.

마을버스는 세 정거장 남았는데
주머니 안에 봉지를 확인하는데

작은 갈비 세 조각을 만져 보아요.

Late Snack

On my way home, I think of Aery,
A little puppy, waiting for me
On the sofa in the living room.

I left the living room curtains open,
So light comes in from the windows,

The living room won't be very dark.
His eyes may hold fear, however.

I bring snack to give it to Aery
Wrapping it in a bag with two folds,
Keeping it in my pocket.

The town bus has three stops left.
I am checking the bag in the pocket
Touching pieces of baked ribs in it.

강아지 바나나

바나나 한 다발은 5개인데
너무 크지 않은 것을 골라요

며칠 동안 두고 먹어야 되니
완전히 노랗게 익지 않은
파르스름한 다발을 골라요.

언제 송이기 말한 적이 있는데

강아지 꼬물이 과일을 먹는데
조금씩 바나나 먹여도 된다고

벌써 꼬물이도 흥분되어서
낼름낼름 받아서 삼켜요.

연하고 기다란 바나나는
긴 다리 꼬물이에게 어울려요.

Puppy's Banana

A bunch of bananas is 5 pieces,
I pick one that isn't too big.

For eating for a few days,
I choose a bunch, not fully yellow
But a bluish one.

Songhee, a little girl, would say
The puppy would eat fruits
Including a little amount of banana.

The puppy is already excited
Wishing to take and swallow it.

The soft and long bananas
Well become a long-legged puppy.

그리운 송이 언니

아파트 베란다 탁자에 올라가면
창밖이 내려다 보여요.

저녁 바람이 불고 있는데
저 아래 나무들이 요란하게 흔들려요.

남쪽 산 너머 하늘은 푸르고 푸른데
그곳에 송이 언니가 있을거예요.

작년 여름에 송이 언니와
거실 베란다에서 서쪽 하늘을 보았어요.

언니가 저를 가만히 안았는데
저 꼬물이는 언니 손가락을 핥고
언니는 꼬물이 턱을 톡톡 두드렸어요.

서쪽으로 해 넘어가는데
저는 눈이 부셔서 지그시 감았어요.

언니는 말했어요
"꼬물아 졸립구나."

저는 말했어요
"아니에요, 송이 언니."

그때 저를 안고 있는 언니 가슴은
포근하고 따스했어요

오늘도 송이 언니는 꼬물이를 생각하나요
오늘도 꼬물이는 송이 언니를 그리워해요

(강아지 꼬물이의 언니에 대한 그리움)

Missing My Sister

Climbing the table on the veranda,
I look out the window.

The evening wind is blowing,
The trees below are swaying noisily.

Beyond the mountain to the south,
The sky is blue and blue,
Where my sister, Songhee stays.

Last summer we looked up the sky
On the veranda of the living room.

You hugged me quietly;
I licked your fingers with my tongue;
You softly tapped on my chin.

As the sun goes down westward,
I was dazzled, gently closed my eyes.

My sister said, "You are sleepy."
I said, "No, Songi, my lovely sister."

At that time, your chest holding me
Was cozy and warm.

Today do you remember me?
Today, I miss you, my sister.

(Puppy's longing for his sister, past owner)

강아지 비

한여름 한밤중에
강아지가 움짓 놀라서
작은 두 귀를 바로 세우고

멀리서 천둥소리가
우둥둥둥 들려오고

강아지가 움짓 일이나서
창가로 바르르 뛰어가니

무거운 빗방울이
우수수 떨어지네요.

Puppy Rain

In the middle of the summer night,
The puppy is startled,
Straighten her little ears.

A sound of thunder in the distance
Is heard, booming.

The puppy gets up,
Runs to the window.

Heavy raindrops
Are falling with wrinkles.

젖은 손수레

큰 빗줄기 가라앉자마자
할아버지는 젖은 모자를 들고
건물 처마에서 일어나서는
다시 손수레를 끌고 가는데

대충 덮어 놓은 수레 안에
종이 상자와 휴지 더미는
빗물에 흠뻑 젖어 들었어요.

할아버지는 지나는 비를 맞으며
수레를 끌고서 지나가는데

한여름 빗줄기 내리면서
도로를 흠뻑 적시고
무거운 수레도 흠뻑 적시고

할아버지 바지를 적시고
누군가 마음도 적시고

A Wet Cart

As the heavy rain subsides
A grandpa holding a wet hat
Rises from the eaves of the building
And pulls the cart again.

In a roughly covered cart
Paper boxes and piles of waste
Are drenched in the rain.

The grandpa in the passing rain
Passes by carrying the cart.

As the summer rain falls,
It drenches all streets
And grandpa's heavy cart.

It also wets grandpa's pants
And wets someone's heart.

한밤중 빗소리

한밤중에 내리는 비는
한참이나 지나서도 여전한데

창문에 부딪히면서
타닥 타닥 타닥

울타리 뽕나무 잎사귀에 내리며
투둑 투둑 투둑

먼 산 너머에서 천둥소리
우둥 우둥 우둥둥

한밤중에 강아지는
두 손에 턱을 내려두고서
가만히 빗소리 들어요.

Raining at Midnight

Drops of rain at midnight
Are still falling for a long time,

Hitting the window glass
Crackle crackle,

Falling on the leaves of mulberry tree
Thud thud thud.

Thunders over the distant mountains
Boom boom boom boom.

A puppy in the middle of the night
Quietly listens to the rain
With his chin resting on his hands.

갑자기 더위

아파트 마을버스 정거장에서
공원 길과 어린이 놀이터가
너무나도 조용합니다

댕댕이 데리고 산책하는 모습은
여러 날 동안 보이지 않아요

댕댕이들도 혀를 늘어뜨리고
쫄랑거리다가 주저앉았어요.

매일 이맘때 놀이터 소란하던
아이들 소리도 들리지 않으니
무거운 더위입니다.

답답하여 뛰어나오던 아이들도
아파트 현관까지 나오다가
다시 집 안으로 들어갔어요.

A Sudden Heat

From the bus stop at the back gate
To the park and kid's playground,
The apartment is so quiet.

Taking a dog for a walk
Can not be seen for days.

Puppies hanging out their tongues
May surrender wandering around.

Even the kids' usual noisy
Can't be heard at the gardens
Because of heavy heat in a day.

Kids running out of impatience
Stop at the doorsteps of apartment.
And go back into their home.

복숭아 색깔

한쪽 볼이 불그레 하고
꼬투리가 붉기도 하고
양쪽 볼이 불그레 하지만

꼭지가 붉지는 않아요.

복숭아 하나하나 마다
얼굴에 조금이라도
붉은 빛을 띠는데

속살도 붉게 닮아가는데
복숭아 색깔입니다.

The Peach Color

One cheek is red
The pods are red too,
Both cheeks are red.

The top is not yet red.

Each peach in branches
Even a bit on the face
Wears a tint of red.

Even the inside of the flesh
Becomes red, the peach color.

무더위 소리

타오르는 무더위는
이른 아침부터 대기를 데우고

나무 그림자도 데워서
새소리도 없고

숲길도 데워서
바람도 불지 않고

골짜기도 데워서
물도 흐르지 않고

타오르는 무더위 속에는
아무런 소리도 들리지 않아요.

The Sound of Heat

The blazing heat
From early in the morning
Is warming the air.

On the shadows of the trees
No birds sing.

In the forest road
No wind blows.

In the warming valley
No water flows.

In the blazing heat
No sound can be heard.

지친 강아지

한동안 아장아장 앞서가다가
언덕길도 깡총깡총 오르더니

비스듬한 내리막길인데도
발걸음이 점점 느려지고
빨간 혀가 질질 늘어지고
고개도 수그리게 되는데

뒤뚱뒤뚱 조금 더 걷다가
바로 그대로 멈추어 서고는
뒤에 오는 나를 쳐다보는데

양쪽 귀까지 벌어진 입 안에
새빨간 혀는 위로 꼬부라져서
할딱 할딱 할딱

까만 눈으로 말하는데
이제 좀 앉아달라고 하는데

저 아래 길가까지 만이라도
잠시라도 안아 달라고

팔에 안긴 3.3킬로 강아지는
입을 널찍하게 벌리고 말하는데
무더위를 버티기 어렵다고

A Tired Puppy

For a while, she toddles ahead,
Climbing up the hill.

After a while, she's on a downhill;
Her steps are getting slower,
Her red tongue is hanging out,
She also shakes her head down.

After toddling a little more,
Soon stopping her steps there,
She's looking at me from behind.

In her mouth open to both ears,
Her bright red tongue curled up,
Clap Clap Clap Clap

She speaks with black eyes;
Please hug me up right now.

Even down to the roadside.
To hug me for a while.

The 3.3kg puppy in my arms
With her mouth wide open
Says she can't stand the heat.

가을바람 강아지

이제 따스한 햇살이
창문 깊게 내리비추고
바람도 선선하게 들어오니

창가에 서성이던 강아지도
그곳에 자리를 잡아요.

감기는 눈을 흔들어대며
햇살 목욕 즐기고

보숭 보숭 털은
살랑살랑 부풀어 일어나서
바람 목욕을 즐겨요.

가을 햇살 받으며
가을 바람 마주하며
졸린 강아지는 일어나지 않아요.

A Puppy in Fall

Now the warm sun
Shines down the window deeply,
The wind come in coolly.

The puppy by the window
Takes a seat there.

Shaking her closed eyes,
She is enjoying a sun bath.

Her soft hair
Gently swells and wakes up
Enjoying a wind bath.

In the autumn sun,
Facing the autumn wind,
The sleepy puppy won't wake up.

3부 우울한 댕댕이
A Blue Puppy

우울한 눈빛

꼬물이 눈을 보면 아는데
검은 두 눈이 말하고 있어요.

그때 무슨 일을 겪었는지
우울한 사연을 담고 있어요.

혼자 있을 때에도
함께 있을 때에도

앉아 있을 때에도
누워 있을 때에도

수시로 앞발을 깨물고
기다란 뒷발도 깨물어요.

손마다 발마다 축축하고
파랗게 멍이 들기도 하지요.

물끄러미 쳐다보는 검은 눈은
쓸쓸하고 초조하게 보이는데
애처로운 사연이 담겨 있어요

꼬물이 눈길을 받아주며 말해요

꼬물이 눈에 담긴 어두움이
어서 지워지기를 바란다고

The Blue Glance

When I look into his eyes
Two black eyes are saying to me.

What happened to him then,
It contains a sad story.

Even when he is alone,
Even when we are together,
Even when he is sitting,
Even when he is lying down,

He bites his front paws,
Even bites his long hind legs.

Every hand and foot remains wet,
Sometimes get blue bruise.

Black eyes staring blankly at me
Look lonely and anxious,
Carry a sad stories of the past.

Taking his blue eyes, I tell him.

"The darkness in your eyes
Would be erased soon with me."

댕댕이 걍걍걍

일주일이나 장마비 내리고
온종일 집 안에 있으니
답답하여 짜증나기도 하여.

엘리베이터 문이 스르르 열려도
누군가 살짝 지나가도
멍멍멍

발자국 소리가 나지 않아도
부스럭 소리 나지 않아도
워워 엉엉엉

주의 주면서 달래보아도
으엉으엉 걍걍걍

우쭐하여 소란 떨면서
앵앵앵 걍걍걍

The Puppy Noises

It rains for a week or so,
Staying at home all day
Is tiring, annoying for a puppy.

The elevator door slides open,
Even someone may pass by,
Mong-mong, Mong-mong.

Even without footsteps,
Even without any rustling,
Wow, Wow, Wow.

Even soothing his feeling,
Eung-eung, Gyang-gyang

Being puffed up, making a fuss
Aeng-aeng, Gyang-gyang

장대비 근심

부슬비 내리면
정감에 촉촉 젖어 들고

소나기 쏟아지면
슬픔에 잠시 잠기는데

장대비 퍼부으니
근심에 흠뻑 젖어 드는데

장대비 퍼부어도
근심은 씻겨나지 않아요.

An Anxious Rain

When it drizzles,
It drenches in my emotion.

When a shower falls,
It would lead me in sad mood.

A heavy rain pours,
And carries me with worry.

Once it pours down,
Worries don't wash away.

늦은 밤 언니 방

톡톡톡 소리가 들려서
얼핏 깨어보니 밤비가 내려요.

창가로 가려고 하는데
언니 방문에 불빛이 새어 나와요.

언니는 밤비 내리는 줄 모르고
지금 시험공부를 하고 있어요.

앞발로 언니 방을 두드리려다가
그냥 발을 내리고 돌아서요.

이제 밤비가 지나가려 하니
저는 이제 웅크리고 자려고요.

송이 언니도 포근히 잠들도록
창밖의 밤비도 살며시 내리기를

A Room at Midnight

With the sound, tok tok tok,
The night rain wakes me up,

When I tries to go to the window,
A light leaks through your door.

She doesn't realize the rain,
Studying for a test right now.

Trying to knock on her room,
I puts my paw down, turns around.

Now that the rain is about to stop,
I'm going to sleep crouched myself.

Hoping Songhee, my sister, sleeps
Peacefully with soft night rain..

기다란 목과 다리

목이 길면 서늘할까요.
목이 짧으면 서늘할까요.

다리가 길면 서늘할까요.
다리가 짧으면 서늘할까요.

목이 길거나 다리가 길거나
목이 짧거나 다리가 짧거나

어렵기는 마찬가지 일거예요.

바로 꼬물이가 그렇거든요.

목과 다리가 길기도 하지만
목과 다리가 짧기도 하지만

서늘하다고 말하지 않아요.

Long Neck and Legs

Would it be cool if the neck is long?
Would it be cool if the neck is short?

Would it be cool if the legs are long?
Would it be cool if the legs are short?

Long neck or long legs,
Short neck or short legs,
It will be difficult as well.

That's what a puppy is like.

Though the neck and legs are long,
Though the neck and legs are short
He's not saying it's cool.

꼬물이 찔끔

꼬물이는 기쁘면 발발발
흥분하면 팔딱팔딱 거리고
그러다가 찔끔 쉬 하는데

소파 위로 팔딱 올라가서
자기 자리 아래 쪽에다가
어쩌다가 찔끔찔끔 하지요.

습관을 고쳐주려고
반듯하게 앉혀놓고서
손으로 가리키며 말해요.

안돼 안돼 이거 안돼요.

꼬물이는 의아해 하다가
검은 눈을 조금 내리고서
자기 집으로 슬며시 들어가요.

Making a Little Pee

When the puppy is happy
And so excited, it flutters,
Then making a little pee.

Jumping up on the sofa,
Under the her seat there,
She would make a little pee.

To teach her manners,
Seating her right there,
Point with my hand and say;
No, No, No, any more.

While the puppy is wondering,
With her black eyes down,
She sneaks into her house.

다시 집으로

현관을 나가려고 하면
어느새 후다닥 뛰어오는데

손바닥을 세우고 표시하는데
"꼬물이 안돼요."

잘록한 허리를 구부리고
다시 자기 자리로 돌아가요.

기죽은 모습이 안스러워서
다시 집으로 되돌아가요.

현관 들어가자마자
폭죽처럼 뛰어오르는데

바로 안아서 품어주면
꼬물이 마음이 풀어져요.

Back Home

When I try to leave the porch
He's already running behind.

I raise my hand and show;
"No, my little boy."

Then bending his narrow waist,
He goes back to his place.

Then I feel sorry for his looking,
Soon I go back home.

As soon as I enter the front door,
He's jumping like a firecracker.

As soon as I hold and hug him,
His heart is relaxed soon.

크림색 별

밤하늘 별들이
반짝인다고 하는데

저 호수 물결도
반짝인다고 하는데

아름다운 연인의 눈빛도
반짝인다고 하는데

누군가 말하고 있어요.

가만히 앉아있는
꼬물이 눈빛도 반짝인다고

다듬지 않은 꼬물이 털빛도
크림색으로 반짝인다고

A Cream Colored Star

Stars in the night sky
Are shining.

The waves in the lake
Are also shining.

The eyes of a beautiful lover
Are shining, too.

Someone says even the eyes
Of a puppy sitting still
Are also twinkling.

His untrimmed cream hair
Is shining like a star.

불안한 아기

강쥐 아기는 얌전하게
기다리지 않지요.

아기는 불안한가 본데
좀처럼 한 시라도
가만히 기다릴 수 없어요.

아빠 엄마를
언니 오빠를
어서 보아야 하는데

아기의 새까만 눈에
눈물이 흐르지 않지만
기다리는 눈빛은 초조해요.

An Anxious Baby

A baby puppy in a room
Won't wait someone quietly.

A baby puppy looks anxious,
Rarely, even for a minute
Can't wait someone quietly.

A puppy hopes to see
Dad and mom,
Or brother and sister
As soon as it can.

In its black eyes
Though no tears do flow,
They do show impatient.

거실을 나가며

한여름 불타는 열기로
거실은 저녁까지 데워지겠고
그대로 나갈 수는 없어서

거실 커튼을 반 정도 닫아서
거친 햇빛을 막아 두고
작은 베란다 통로만 열고서

거실 안 유리문도 닫고서
냉방 조절을 해 놓고서 나가요.

서늘하게 유지되는 실내에
꼬마 댕댕이 두고서 안심해요.

Leaving the Place

Since the burning heat of midsummer
Will warm the living room till evening,
I can't go out as it is.

Closing the living room curtain half,
Blocking the harsh sunlight,
Opening a small veranda hole,

Closing the glass door in the living room,
Turning on the air conditioner,
I can go out.

In the cool living room,
A little puppy will be safe and cool.

빗방울 소리

창가에 부딪히고
틱틱 티디 딕

나뭇잎에 떨어지고
툭툭 투두 둑

길가 바위에 튀기고
토독 토도 독

강아지 코에도
빗방울 떨어지며
코고 코고 곡

The Raindrops

Hitting the window
Tick tick tick tick

Falling on leaves
Tuk tuk todu duk

Splashing on pathway rocks
Todok todo todok

Falling on puppy's nose
Kogo kogo gok

짙어지는 계절

산이 짙어지고 짙어지면
녹색은 검게 되고

깊이 들어가고 들어가면
어두운 숲에 둘러싸이고

길도 보이지 않고
숲도 보이지 않고

아무것도 보이지 않고
나도 보이지 않고

The Thick Color

When the color of mountain
Gets thicker and thicker,
Green turns black.

If you go deep and deep,
Surrounded by dark forest.

The path cannot be seen;
The forest cannot be seen.

Nothing can be seen;
Nor can myself be seen.

아름다운 모습

털 깍기 하고 나서
너의 모습을 보면

긴 다리에 오똑 솟아난 귀들
둥 위로 말려진 복술 꼬랑지

톡 튀어나온 검은 코
동그란 검은 눈

바라보는 검은 눈으로
무슨 이야기를 하나요.

꼬물이 온몸에는
많은 이야기가 있어요.

A Beautiful Look

After trimming hair,
Your drawings are

Protruding ears with long legs,
A hairy tail rolled over back,

A bulging black nose,
Round black eyes.

With your black eyes,
What stories are you talking about?

You holds lots of stories to tell
All over your body.

우울한 과거

이제 한바탕 장난도 그치고
물렁 삐빅이 인형을 던져두고

나비 리본 허수아비도
바닥에 팽개쳐 두어요.

옆으로 드러누워서
앞다리 뒷다리 길게 뻗이요.

돌돌 말려진 꼬랑지를
길게 풀어 놓아요.

한창 쫑긋했던 두 귀도
조금 접어 놓아요.

오늘 밤부터 지나간 일들
아픈 사연을 잊어야 하지요.

Gloomy Past Memories

Stopping playing around now,
Throwing a soft calling doll away,
Throwing a butterfly doll on the floor,

Lying sideways on the sofa,
He stretches out front and hind legs.

Letting a rolled-up tail get loosen,
Even two moving ears fold a bit.

The sad memories that he has had
Should be erased after tonight.

기다림

누가 오기를 기다리며
두 손과 두 발을 모으고
지루하게 기다려요.

한참 지나고 나서
두 발을 쭉 뻗고서

이제 두 손도 펴고서
지루하게 기다려요.

지금이라도 들어와서
창문을 닫아주고 나서

살며시 쓰다듬어 주고
포근하게 안아주기를

Waiting for Someone

Waiting for someone to come,
Putting both hands and feet together,
He is waiting dully.

After a good while,
With both feet outstretched,
With both hands open,
He is waiting boringly.

The puppy is waiting for someone
Who will come in soon,
Close the window,

Gently caring for his head,
And hugging him with warmth.

장마 코스모스

비에 흠뻑 젖어 늘어져도
빗물 맞아 쓰러져도
빗물에 휩쓸려 부러져도

짙푸른 코스모스
피어나기 시작해요.

안개 거두어지지 않아도
새하얀 코스모스

햇살 기다리지 않고도
새빨간 코스모스

A Cosmos in Rain

Though drenched in the rain,
Fallen down in the rain,
Swept away by the rain,

A deep blue cosmos
Starts to bloom in the fence.

Though the mist does stay,
Pure white cosmos.

Without waiting for sunlight,
Bright red cosmos.

가을 풀벌레

이곳 어디에서인가
이상한 소리가 들리는데

끊임없이 들리는 소리는
소란하지 않으니
성가시지도 않아요.

한밤에는 더 심하고
숲에서는 더 심한데
소란하지도 않아요.

풀벌레 소리가 들리는데
가을을 말하고 있어요.

Autumn Bugs

Somewhere else
A strange noise is heard.

The lasting sound
Is not fuss at all,
Even not annoyed.

In the midnight,
Even in the forest,
The sound is getting more.

The sound of grass bugs
Tells me stories of autumn.

함께 가기로

꼬물이 강쥐에게 물어보아요.
"혼자서 갈 수 있겠니?"

대답 없이 쳐다보기만 해요.
무슨 말인지도 모르니까요.

한동안 어리둥절하다가
살짝 뛰어올리서

가슴에 발을 딛으며
얼굴을 날름날름 핥아요.

가슴에 안겨서 자리를 잡는데

혼자서 갈 수 없다고 하면서
함께 가자고 쳐다보아요.

Going Together

I quietly ask the puppy,
"My little kid, can you go alone?"

She stares at me without answering,
For she doesn't realize what I mean.

Bewildered for a while,
She lightly jumps up to me.

Stepping on my chest,
She licks and licks my face.

Cuddling up to my chest,
She takes her place there.

Saying she can't go alone,
She looks at me to go with me.

댕댕이 이발기

내일 댕댕이 털을
예쁘게 다듬어야 하는데

바리캉 소리에 놀라서
비명 지르지 말아야 하기에

오늘 밤 댕댕이 잠자리 옆에
이발기를 두어요.

낮에 물고 놀던 나비인형 옆에
이발기를 두어요.

내일 바리캉 소리에
보채지 말아야 하기를

The Hair Clipper

To trim puppy's hair tomorrow
Needs to make her pretty.

Being startled by the clipping noisy,
She should not scream.

Tonight, next to the puppy bed,
Place a hair clipper.

Next to the butterfly doll
She would play with during the day,
Place a hair clipper.

Tomorrow, due to the clipping noisy,
She wouldn't be annoyed.

댕댕이 미용

겨울을 준비해야 하니
털을 바싹 깎지는 말고
슬며시 다듬어야 합니다.

꽁무니는 짧고 토실하게
꽁지는 둥글게 다듬어서
깜찍하게 살려내야 합니다.

기다란 다리가 날씬해 보이게
미리 재어보고 달래고 어르고

가슴에 안아서 쓰다듬으면서
털을 자르면서 쳐내야 합니다.

The Puppy Grooming

For winter season to come,
The hair needs trimming,
Not too short smoothing it out.

The hind should be short, plump,
The tail should be trim round,
Which makes her cute.

For her long legs to be slimmer,
Envisaging shape, soothing her.

While being hugged and stroked,
Her hair will be trimmed.

외로운 댕댕이

한나절 쓸쓸히 기다리는데
다시 만나기만을 바래요

온종일 기다리며
조급하여 걱정이 되어요

하루 이틀 지나면
댕댕이 눈빛은 슬퍼지네요

나는 어디로 가야 하는지
나에게 외로움 남겨지겠지.

A Lonely Puppy

He is lonely waiting for half a day
Hoping to see his mother again.

Waiting all day long,
He is worried and more anxious.

After a day or two,
The puppy's eyes are getting sad.

Where should I go?
Will loneliness leave for me?